The Science of Success

The Science of Success

August Raines

CONTENTS

1

Introduction to Success

Success is important. Organizations and businesses spend vast amounts of time and money to hire, train, and lead their employees, and then reward them for success. Schools are graded on the success of their students. People who are successful are often treated differently by their friends, family, and colleagues. They may be seen as more intelligent, more powerful, and more talented. Success has been built on diligence and hard work, which are a necessary part of learning and growing. Without natural talent or skills, success is still possible through education and training.

People are motivated by a variety of factors, including culture, age, and personality. If you want to motivate someone, you can identify their strongest desires and not expect these to change easily. The need for success in order to gain respect from others is a basic desire. Parents and teachers recognize student achievements and special talents. Many of us work hard on the job to impress the boss. Not only money, but success on the job by solving problems or being part of a winning team, are strong motivators. We may spend long hours at the gym or in the studio trying to create the perfect body, perfect jump shot, or perfect voice. We are driven to be perfect and successful, and yet we may never actually achieve our dream.

Defining Success

If you do not understand what you value most, you may pursue the wrong goals or may not be satisfied with what you achieve. For example, many people start off striving for a high salary or prestigious job title, only to find that these did not lead to satisfaction. Therefore, before you can possibly become truly successful, you must first define what success actually means to you. Consider the following questions in order to understand your own definition of success: What are the three or four most satisfying moments of your life so far? How did you achieve these moments and what did they have in common? What advice about living a successful life would you give your grandchild? Can you think of three or four successful people who do not get much public recognition but are happy with their lives?

When people think of success, they often think of things that appeal to public perception, such as power, status, or wealth. However, to be truly successful, it is important to identify first what you as an individual find meaningful. Exactly what constitutes a successful life or career varies from person to person. When striving for success, it is critical to understand your own aspirations. This is an important step for career planning and your own professional development. How you define success also affects how you measure success. For example, if you value public recognition, you may work to become the most influential person in your field. On the other hand, if you value personal happiness more, you may have more meaningful interactions with family and friends.

The Importance of Setting Goals

They are subjective, so do not hesitate to set very high, demanding, self-demanding, ambitious objectives. A man without any goals is not an alive human being but an animal, a puppet; in observing them from the outside, we should be able to recognize that their life is a rational life. Some people know that they are not realizing their true potential, and they persevere doing what they know is bad for their lives. They do not have a consciousness of how important their trajectory is and are therefore unaware of their lack of happiness and personal security. They deceive professionals and managers of organizations into accepting them and are getting each year a little closer to the level of mediocrity they have chosen. These weak-minded individuals use every means, some of them not very ethical, to seek praise and recognition that is not due to them. They need to distinguish between humility and lack of self-esteem. Sometimes reaching your goal is not that important, do not forget that the journey (what is it that you will do to get to your objective?) is what is most exciting. Use your goals to make you grow.

If our goals are not specific and measurable, we cannot determine exactly how much effort we need to expend in order to accomplish them. "I want to be happy." "I want to be rich." These are examples of general, abstract goals. It is important to be self-demanding, realistic, and specific. To set correct goals, we have to ask the following questions: What? When? How? Where? We should not only establish all the specific and long-term goals that we want to accomplish in each of the main areas of our lives but should also establish short-term objectives for the purpose of obtaining them. The top executives in the country have a clear understanding of how important goals are.

2

Psychology of Success

As noted by Hogan, Wallach and Wallach, self-efficacious people regard difficult activities as tasks to be mastered and therefore gain intrinsic interest and satisfaction from them. People with self-confidence try harder, set challenging goals, and persevere longer. Hanvey found that people with a high sense of personal responsibility readily seek and accept conditions through which they can exercise personal control-power and they prefer to be agents of their own fate rather than objects of the will of others. The evidence is huge: people who perceive themselves as capable and as in control work harder and succeed.

Comstock suggested that mental readiness is extremely important. "To maintain a healthy goal orientation," he recommended, "the individual must sustain an atmosphere of growth and must tolerate the frustration and setbacks that accompany new means-ends relations."

The psychology of achievement involves more than just personal abilities - personal knowledge of success strategies is also key. Bandura developed a theory of self-efficacy in which he proposed that people who believe they are capable of bringing about desired changes accomplish more than people who do not. A person's psychological readiness for a change predicts a major part of whether the change will be successful. People who achieve are not just of higher ability, however one defines that complex term. They are people who are convinced that they can, in fact, achieve their goals. They believe that they are responsible for their own destinies and they believe that they can bring about desired achievements.

Motivation and Persistence

The objective of the scientist of adulthood can only be to contribute to the insights about successful functionings that adults themselves can use to increase their day-to-day effectiveness and their sense of satisfaction.

The search for success principles has been made difficult by willing assumptions, beliefs, and aspirations that cloud efforts to get people to see their lives as they really live them - and more importantly, to become more successful. We stress, then, the importance for all - but especially for those who seek knowledge from the research - to give up any pretense of contextual objectivity, that is, of standing outside the boundaries of one's subject matter to make clean, clever, clinical, uninvolved statements.

New studies of principles of successful people show a correlation, not a cause and effect relationship - what you think of yourself and life can help influence what you become.

Succeeding in life without a manual: The scientific study of adults succeeding in a variety of areas of life sheds light on keys to success in a society where the highest reward goes not to those who have the richest farm fields, but to producers in other areas of economic, political, and artistic endeavor. Success in adulthood is the result of a combination of events, activities, and characteristics that are thought to develop as the developing person in interaction with the settings in which they find themselves.

Mindset and Belief Systems

There have been numerous examples and research investigating the role that our specific mindset or belief system around achievement, intelligence, or other traits can have on our success in those areas. It has been illustrated in several studies that those individuals who have a growth mindset in an area, or those who believe that the traits or qualifications of success can be developed and that areas such as intelligence and achievement can be cultivated, are more likely to achieve success in that area. Individuals who believe and have a fixed mindset that these areas are traits that cannot be changed or improved upon are more likely to experience failure or give up when confronted with a challenge or situation where the trait is called into question. Individuals who hold these fixed beliefs in their intelligence and other traits cannot change it and fail to develop coping strategies to recover from failure; this leads to the development of a fragile sense of self.

Just as our attitudes and beliefs about ourselves can shape our behavior and experiences, the mindset that we have in any area of our life can have a significant impact on our levels of success and achievement. One of the most popular areas of research currently on the science of success is focused on the concept of "mindset" and the critical role that our belief system has in how we approach our goals in life. Our specific mindset in any area can contribute significantly to whether we are successful and the degree to which we can create and take advantage of opportunities and overcome adversity and challenges in our pursuit of achievement.

3

Strategic Planning

Your action plan and list of priorities need to be mutually exclusive and exhaustive. They are independent of one another, but they cover everything in your life. This will help you to disconnect from those to-do lists bouncing around your head and help you relax more. Every task on your lists needs a start time, an end time, and a budget. For those needing completion within a particular time frame, ensure the deadline is stated, as this influences prioritization. All tasks needing to be completed at a particular time are also milestones or waypoints that will need to be factored into your initial action plan. This includes time for each phase of the project, work that cannot be overlapping, concurrent with other tasks, and that is dependent upon completion of a predecessor or successor. Finally, all resources need accounting for, including staffing, physically completing the work, travel time, etc. Every person involved in a task other than the number one priority should be assigned that task only.

An action plan is the roadmap we use to get from where we are standing to where we want to arrive. Our mind and our nervous system are designed to give us certainty. If we are aiming at a target, everything about our body language, our physiology, the way we speak and think is designed to give us certainty in the steps we are taking. That, in turn, instills confidence. Can you imagine if you got on a plane, and in the cockpit you saw the pilots with their heads in their hands? "We've never been this flight path before," they wail. "We don't know how to fly to New York. I've never done this before. Can anybody help us?" Plan the target and plan the steps to get there.

SWOT Analysis

The strengths and weaknesses focus on internal factors that contribute to business success or failure, while opportunities and threats deal with external factors not usually influenced by the company. In business, a SWOT analysis can identify the difference between where the organization is compared to its goals and where it has to be or wants to be. It also matches strengths to opportunities, so that the organization can take advantage of opportunities by using strengths. It meshes weaknesses and threats, which develop strategies to avoid or minimize them.

SWOT stands for strengths, weaknesses, opportunities, and threats. Many organizations and companies use SWOT analysis to assess their competitive position, estimate how they will maintain their competitive strength, and thus create a plan to help the organization achieve its objectives. By performing SWOT analysis, companies can identify both how well their company is performing and what is needed to keep and maintain a leading position. If it isn't possible to take advantage of a new opportunity, doing SWOT analysis can lead the company to take actions to reduce these gaps. SWOT analysis is a "snapshot" of a company's position and the strategy it needs to define and implement for the future. This tool is beneficial in making decisions and solving problems because it helps company leaders and staff members to focus on what they do well, and where they can improve.

SMART Goals

In reality, people are likely to feel comfortable with challenges if they have the ability and resources available to achieve them. A goal that is specific helps in developing the ability, new skills, and competencies as well as resources in order to meet it. In addition, it also acts as a positive frame of reference to improve the work, rather than as a primary source of stress. When a manager sets goals for his subordinates, he should always ensure that their goals complement the overall objectives of the company. If not, in stress, subordinates might ignore aspects of their role that have not been included in their goal, even if they are critical.

Mnemonics are strategies for remembering and help us to organize information for better recall. SMART is a mnemonic for setting effective goals. According to its methodology, good goals should be specific, measurable, assignable, realistic, and time-related. When it comes to setting and achieving goals, this framework is highly useful. Goals that are specific are more likely to be achieved. When goals clearly state 'what' is involved, and there is less ambiguity about what is intended, people understand exactly what is expected of them. They also become highly motivated to deliver the outcome.

4

Productivity and Time Management

Considering this, what else can be the best productivity strategy that you can use?

This productivity method respects your time, forces you to fix a schedule, lets work with you and not against you, makes you decide what is important and what is not, and makes you aware of your obligations. You naturally start to optimize the available time. This method is working top-down and bottom-up. This may sound like the opposite of flexibility and adaptability, but it is not. Flexibility is not a job, but the process is not. Flexibility is one of the most crucial entrepreneurial skills, but not in planning your daily work. Small business has to be flexible in the market. It is not. The process might be.

In order to implement hourly time blocking, it is appropriately challenging. It is required from you to have top-down awareness on how to spend your day and self-awareness in a bottom-up way, to know how much time every activity takes.

With hourly time blocking, you naturally eliminate the menial activities - low-value actions - from your day due to your time constraints. Finally, even if you can't eliminate all distractions, when you know that you have to work on a project for 2 hours, it becomes much easier to avoid these distractions altogether.

Prioritization Techniques

But the overall problem of managing professional and personal life can't be ignored. Otherwise, we risk not effectively reaching any of the potential goals we long to accomplish, succumbing to constant fatigue, or, at the very least, not being able to enjoy the fruits of our labors. Perhaps it's because I need help with time management myself that I've learned about a number of tools and techniques that can address this problem. This chapter is a brief overview of some of my favorite methods, intended to give you the incentive to look more deeply into these subjects if time management is an issue for you. With a few simple techniques, you can prioritize whatever professional and personal goals are important to you.

Given that long-term objectives typically require consistent effort over time, it's essential to manage your workload to ensure that real progress is made toward completing them. This, in turn, generally requires the effective completion of shorter-term tasks. One problem, though, is that most individuals have a large number of things that they could work on at any given time. There are always more potential tasks than we have the capacity to complete. As a result, for several months, we may find that we are in an 'emergency' mode in which both long-term objectives and shorter-term tasks are given equal priority.

Effective Scheduling

It is well established that using a time management system provides us with more time and less stress, improves our ability to fulfill our own desires and goals, and increases our overall performance. Of the different strategies we can employ, there are nine key concepts that have repeatedly been found to be associated with increased performance and personal effectiveness. In this chapter, you will find help on how to apply these concepts to your life and your schedule.

1. Monitor your time: The most accurately different people say they can estimate time is three hours in advance. We often get stuck in the here and now of what we are doing and can easily overestimate or underestimate the amount of time we are spending on a task.

2. Simplicity of schedule: Research shows that in any week, an average person can cope effectively with one or two major ongoing projects.

3. Starting and stopping leisure time: Try to fit your work around leisure time rather than leisure time around work.

4. Concentration periods: We generally have three to four-hour periods during a day when our bodies are at their peak of alertness and effectiveness, and our energy levels are highest.

5. Workspace: With workplaces becoming increasingly open, it is harder to find space for quiet, focused work. For tasks that require concentration, consider creating an alternative space to work.

5

Building Resilience

When you find that all your effort and skills cannot overcome an obstacle, it can be helpful to remember that some things are not within your control. Certainly, you can try to influence and change outcomes, but sometimes all you can do is influence the way you react to the situation. It may seem counterintuitive that letting go of your plan for maintaining happiness is a good way to build resilience, but a consistent adjustment to the fact that not everything will go your way actually helps you be flexible and cope with new challenges. This way of coping is known as a coping style, which is often referred to as characteristic of the person and something that can be learned through training.

Resilience is the capacity to bounce back when things don't go the way you had planned. Being resilient in tough times doesn't require strength or huge amounts of courage, but the ability to think and respond flexibly. It's letting go of your plans and coming up with new plans. Things that lead to resilience include finding meaning in life, continually readjusting your plan for happiness, getting enough mental and physical rest, eating well, and building emotional connections.

Coping with Failure

It is these aforementioned small realistic sub-goals that will scaffold the quality of our lives. First, they have to be realistic. We should not plan to clean our houses, tell ourselves that if we do A, then B, then C, and so forth, those houses will become clean. On the other hand, if the house has not seen a mop in years, one goal of the next chore to be done might be to lift up the accumulated dust on a broom or something. Are our goals measurable? How do we know we have accomplished them? This is another point of setting puzzles for ourselves. Goals should be intelligible to us, should be as specific as possible, should be built into sub-goals, should be very precise. More course within our aspirations is the assured right path to success. Our goals should be ranked, with the most important goal stated explicitly first. We should ever be aware of the cruciality of the top-ranking most important goal. If we lose the most important goal, we won't know what to do with the others.

It would be naive to attempt success if we were not prepared for failure. Sometimes failure is a learning process – maybe we aim for something unrealistic or maybe we don't approach the problem in the most efficacious manner. But the more frequently failure occurs, the easier it is for the majority of us to despair. We all know despair is the arch villain of effort. The secret of success is the unyielding continuity of purpose and effort. For those of us who have failed many times, the key to continued achievement lies in formulating our goals in ways that abate frustration, that help us face the negative disappointments in our lives. Circumstances will occur in the lives of us all that will suggest failure. We should laugh at the negative evidence, for it does not dictate the future.

Adaptability and Flexibility

The best ways to adapt and become flexible to new circumstances are to prepare yourself for these situations. The more you learn and are aware of, the better prepared you will be to meet the obstacles head-on and adapt to them. Using the adjective "adaptable" rather than "flexible" for those who like hard definitions, it is the ability to change (be adaptable) that an immobilized company or employee may rapidly evolve after being struck down. Flexibility implies that the change happened as an answer to a challenge.

You may have heard the saying, "The typical definition of insanity is doing the same thing over and over again and expecting different results." And the fact is, a large part of our lives—our actions, our work, our relationships, our views—have traditions associated with them. Even simple tasks such as brewing coffee or taking a shower have become rituals in their own right. However, simply doing the same things you've always done won't always yield the same results in the game of life. We often face new and different challenges and obstacles in our road to success. The fact is, you must be prepared to adapt to challenges and changes in the best, most positive way.

6

Interpersonal Skills

Whether we work effectively with others or allow stress to develop is our key, as ineffective communication is one large source of work-related stress. Effective stress management is about achieving a "good" level; this varies from one person to another and concerns how much workload and pressure suits you best. Factors causing stress are those that break your "good" level - any cause of work-related stress will receive as many different and individual reactions as each worker! Therefore, in order to manage stress, you need to ensure that you are personally taking control of the factors that influence these demands. Also, you must identify the link between stress and communication and develop your communication skills in order to reduce the levels and impact of unwanted stress.

Also called social skills or communication skills, interpersonal abilities make it easy for us to work with others easily and without friction. Much of the supervision time is spent in contact with other people, at meetings, during updates, with colleagues, etc. This is time at which each person does things for other people and things are done for him. In other words, communication is extremely complex. Consequently, as important as well-developed communication skills are, they are not the only people-related skills that contribute to successful job performance. Other vital personal attributes include respect for the rights of others, the ability to listen and show empathy, to make decisions, to manage conflicts, to work in groups and respect cultural and ecological matters.

Communication Skills

When you become skilled in these six areas, you will find that doors open for you. Opportunities will appear where few existed before. You will attain a more favorable position with others, management, and your family.

1. Empathy - the ability to see things from another person's point of view. 2. Consideration - thinking about the person to whom you are speaking. What are their interests? Problems? 3. Concreteness - being specific and definite whenever possible. Don't talk in general terms. Be sure to illustrate what you are talking about. 4. Clarity - speaking or writing so that your receiver can understand what you are saying. The information is clear and easy to understand. 5. Impact - your behavior reinforces what you say. Impact is the nonverbal aspect - how you dress, your body language - all reinforced by your attitude. 6. Consistency - the attitude that supports you.

You can develop and improve six specific communication skills to help you sell yourself and your ideas. These six skills are:

The McKinsey study clearly emphasized that communication skills are a must. You must also learn how to "sell" your objectives - how to create a favorable impression. (It also helps to listen to others and make sure that you have a real "dialogue.")

Networking and Relationship Building

Still, I have worked with several successful scientists who are not well connected to the wider community. Some work mainly in large institutions where finding like-minded colleagues is easier than most places, or have staff who do the necessary liaison for them. Some actively avoid time-consuming and distracting association with other researchers, preferring interactions with their own friends, colleagues within their working groups or clients. In all instances, they pay a price. Even in our electronic age, personal contact should not be underestimated. It's more work than emails, but involves far fewer misunderstandings, mistakes, and wasted time. Networking is an important long-term goal. Some people are naturally good at it, but everyone can build their network using modest steps. Even shy people with few social skills can develop a wide network with regular practice. To get started, check who you need to know and/or interact with and spend 10-15 minutes a few times a week talking and listening to the major players. If you want to establish a stronger relationship, find ways to help that person, then do so. If possible, make the help specific and the solution easy to implement, but try to be equally helpful even with minimal understanding.

Networking and managing relationships are the skills that will help you achieve many of your other goals as well. Your network can eventually help you secure a better job, land the big project that requires contributors from multiple disciplines, help you move into new areas entirely, or keep you there. Networking can help you find new clients, partners, staff, suppliers, and the services and information you need to deliver your job at peak capability. These goals and benefits are common to both scientific and other professions.

7 |

Leadership and Influence

Hence the fate of nations depends on the skills and general level of leadership exercised by their citizens. The most challenging test of general leadership is one that has no solutions, the third law of program design. What do you do when there is no objective way of defining success? The third law asserts that goals associated with the third-law category of activity should always be formulated in terms of setting positive examples for other people to follow. This is not to say weaker members of society should receive the same level of compensation for work as more talented and motivated individuals.

What is leadership? I define it as the skill and capacity to design and deliver the future. As parents, teachers, businesspeople, and professionals, all of us can develop and exercise the skills of leadership outlined in this and other books. Indeed, there is no limit to the number of individuals to whom leadership can be taught. In families where the parents are jobless or work long and hard just to gain basic sustenance, children develop into non-leaders bereft of any sense of future possibility. The act of supporting a family is the first lesson, perhaps the most meaningful one, in designing the future for those you love. In every society throughout time, when common people have the resources to look beyond their present circumstances, they exercise the act of leadership by their choices and behavior.

Leading by Example

Watching the executives strive for greatness and improvement, the professionals became inspired to follow suit. The rest of the organizational personnel saw this and realized that our leaders not only talked the talk, they walked the talk. Not long after, several executives started offering training and development as an incentive. The policy was spelled out. There is a company investment in the individual's future in the amount of $500, and as a part of the investment, there is the expectation that the individual agrees to remain with the company for at least two years.

Leaders at all levels of the organization can exert their influence to support and engage the team in training and development opportunities. The executives that I have coached were role models. They scheduled their training program on an annual basis. They were not only committed to their own training, but they also created a budget to support training for their teams. With this, they instilled a culture of continuous improvement within their organizations. From there, it didn't matter whether career development discussions were held with their direct reports, you engage in training or you get out.

Inspirational Leadership

This evidence makes it clear that leadership is not a passive role. Leadership development programs need to be organized in an experiential - active learning - mode. Active leaders are continuous learners. They are self-aware and they benefit from feedback from their constituents. The leadership person in an organization acts as a steward redefining the playing field to allow all the players to be present together. They must help team members develop a sense of identity with the main organization rather than rely on individual performance appraisals and career development programs. As role models, they must demonstrate the organization's values in their own behavior. They must engage in rhetoric and public relations on behalf of the organization to foster a collective commitment to the organization and its goals. The self-knowledge that is so important to success can, therefore, be a trap that makes one a captive of one's own inflexible self-definitions. Indeed, the elegant title of well-endowed children described by Robert Blum is a good one for a considerable number of self-aware individuals; they expect too much because they are used to getting too much. A different kind of self-knowledge might prevent that bind, but only if the world they choose to inhabit placed a premium on the autonomy, respect for diversity, and a balance between personal needs and personal responsibility that underpins self-knowledge.

Scientific research has shown that it is one of the most effective ways of influencing a group to get the best from its members. Inspirational leaders excel at articulating the vision, challenging, empowering, modeling the values, and experimenting. They instill a sense of community, and the resulting atmosphere is lively, challenging, stimulating, dynamic, serious, and open. Oftentimes, successful leaders gave voice to the anger and discomfort of their followers, and they had a lot of heartfelt stories. Leaders who are perceived as compassionate and warm are readily seen as having vision and moral authority. What is striking about these findings is that studies of leadership consistently report that experienced leaders in successful companies discover who they are - their core values and self-imposed rules increase their leadership effectiveness substantially. Previously, it was believed that leaders discovered themselves in the world around them.

Financial Management

It is necessary to evaluate the market structure. Realize that the financial guide can help in the process of searching in small centers. Learn different methods of mortgage financing, especially non-traditional mortgage lending and common methods of purchasing a new or existing home. Learn the importance of using a mortgage calculator. Categorize the details of the list of purchase and acquisition schedules in cost-effective departments. Provide for commission costs. Household builders use real estate trading platforms. Consider various types of rental accommodations, including lease options. Carry out a long-term annual and rent comparison. It is necessary to compare both before and after closing. Wealth management and investments. Learn about profit, annuities, and real estate investments, including the potential for personal and social security as well as net worth. Build a compensation plan to build wealth. Talk to a financial advisor or lawyer about estate planning. Write an informal business proposal related to the personal financial plan.

Compare individual saving and investment instruments including certificates of deposit (CDs), risky higher-yield savings accounts, money market accounts, stocks, and bonds. Credit and investing options. Compare various payment options available and analyze the opportunity cost of deductible, higher-interest rates versus risk. Analyze and create a personal debt-strategy plan to control payday lending decisions. Develop a written financial strategy to include earned income tax, savings, and investment, and grant tax benefits. Understand how credit will provide money in case of emergencies as well as provide personal and family security and social and consumer benefits. Small dollar loans, including medical, household, and education loans, are examined. Discuss incentives for increasing Medical Savings Accounts. Analyze interest-free loans through various incentives such as health savings accounts, education, retirement plans, and disability insurance. Information on long-term care insurance and MassHealth nursing home benefits. Studies on how other forms of life insurance and disability benefits are handled by life insurance companies. Information on the value of insurance management and the flexibility of insurance premiums, coverage, benefits, exclusions, and limitations of homeowners insurance. Discuss the possibility of becoming a homeowner. Find out what real estate agency comparison's information shows. Determine the factors that influence real estate value, including the influence of healthy and safe sites. Flood, earthquake, tornado, hurricane, terrorism, skipped sewer, and other natural disasters can cause death.

Budgeting and Saving

Planning helps you take control because you are setting aside small amounts for unexpected costs, preventing the need to tap into your long-term financial assets. It also helps you determine how much you can safely spend so you do not tap into your long-term assets. Regularly budget money for savings. Try to save money on a regular basis and don't use credit cards except in an emergency. Whenever possible, carry checks or cash instead. When you receive checks, cash, or a paycheck, it is suggested that you consistently budget money to be paid for your living expenses, create an emergency fund, and set aside a portion for short-term and long-term goals. If your living expenses are underestimated, there is a good chance you may use your savings or long-term assets to pay for them. These may include food, housing, utilities, transportation, insurance (medical, auto, homeowners/rental, and life), clothing, fitness memberships, charitable donations, and/or mandatory loan and credit card payments. By giving the impression your rent was either moved to cover your other operating expenses, the chances are that you can pay your rent. However, if you simply cash your paychecks at the time being, you can somehow pay your rent and other operating expenses.

The key to successful money management is a mix of long-term financial planning and short-term, day-to-day money management. Financial planning helps us reach long-term financial goals such as saving for college or large purchases, retirement, vacations, or investments. The act of planning how much to budget or how much to save for these goals is only one part of the process. The planning part is usually the most difficult because it is a long-term activity. Therefore, the day-to-day aspects of managing your money become the other part of the important mix of money management. This is where the fun, as well as the hard work, occurs since day-to-day management helps us maintain financial control and flexibility and helps us pay off our creditors in a timely manner.

Investing for the Future

A clear understanding of what makes an investment attractive can thus be of great value. It can help you assess how well you are doing in relation to other opportunities. It can also guide you in making decisions that best match your special needs and preferences. And it can help you realize it is time to change direction, perhaps because your family or business or children have grown in a way that calls for different investments.

Different people have different values and preferences, and as a result, they have different ways of defining success. But one of the few goals upon which nearly all people can agree is the desire to attract success over the long term. It is impossible to provide for one's material needs and desires today without some thought for the future. Of course, however, we define success, it regularly depends on investing some of today's financial resources in ways that will improve our welfare in the future. Even the young person who cannot imagine old age must invest his or her earnings in some way to avoid the horrors of living in poverty.

9 |

Health and Well-being

Inactivity causes a reduction in neuron growth, ongoing loss of connections, and inefficiency in neurotransmission. Over time, you lose your mental agility. As you age, you could become completely disadvantaged. The reduction in neuron growth can occur after only two weeks of inactivity. With no physical challenge to the body, muscle loss and a decrease in cardiovascular capacity and other physical abilities continue. Your body becomes an unwanted baggage slowing you down. To perform at your peak, you need a healthy brain, body, emotions and spirit. Choose messages that make you feel good. Read out loud messages that make you laugh. Assistance, gratitude and messages that are nurturing provide comfort and healing, boosting physical health and spiritual well-being. Accomplishing the assignments will enable your manager brain to connect to these functions.

The message is clear: managing stress and keeping well-being and resilience high is essential if you wish to be successful. When we experience stress, the stress hormones released reduce our ability to think and perform. When stress is ongoing, it can lead to feelings of despair. These feelings then erode our motivation and self-confidence. Stress and low resilience are common among those of us who are successful. Managing success is essential if you wish to maintain and improve it over time.

Balancing Work and Life

But as soon as people say what sacrifices they are not willing to make for work, they reveal what priorities take precedence over work. Only about 1.2% of people admit that they seriously agree that "Our work suffers because of what we demand" and "Do you wish we had more time off?" A lot more people disagree furiously with these contrary statements. They clearly spend most of their lives at work—and love it. Others grumble. Work cuts peak hours out of daily schedules. People who work cannot also laze about. They can't visit friends. They have to rush decisions about things like family, health, and household chores. Even on days off, there is so much catch-up. Why be impatient with that? It usually means being too immersed in work to remember why we even need days off. After all, weekends may make home life into a full-time hobby.

For most of us, work is part of life. Our jobs hit us hard in the middle of living. But the more you care about your work, the more likely you are to become absorbed in it. The French have a saying for that: "Vive le travail!" If you enjoy your work, you may almost feel deprived if you have to skip it. And do you cut hours of fun to make time for work that is just a job? No, it is not likely. When people are carefully asked to itemize both sides of their weekly time budget, only about 2.2 people out of 100 strongly agree with these statements: "We resent any overtime on the job"; "Work takes up too much of our time." People are even more likely to disagree by a lot with this, "I wish I didn't have to work"; "Work is a waste of time."

Physical and Mental Health Strategies

When it comes to achieving greatness in life, we personally believe that it's more important to be healthy rather than being wealthy. There is no point in having a million bucks if you're dead or bedridden and unable to enjoy the riches. For obvious reasons, your health is the most important factor in achieving any of your life goals. You have only one chance, one life. In it, you have to take advantage of whatever chance that exists to become a lean, strong, and healthy person, regardless of the means or the methods. There are no easy ways. You must take charge of your desired goals and push yourself to the limit. Being physically and mentally fit is the most important factor in your life. But sometimes, with so much work to be done, you tend to forget to take a break to look after yourself. This chapter is a reminder to look after your health and to offer some strategies to ensure that you are treating your body and mind with the care and attention they deserve. We intend to show that anyone can achieve amazing gains in health and fitness, regardless of our chronological age, through minimal time spent on exercise, employing ultra-brief routines, maintaining a low percentage of body fat by employing a minimal amount of time and effort to burn fat, and controlling our diet.

Conclusion and Final Thoughts

There is something for everyone in this book. It has been written for people in general, who are occupied with work and do not have much time to read, but have a keen interest in learning. The book does not demand formal training, i.e. advanced cultural, scientific or technical knowledge. If it is demagogic, it is so by design – to build fundamental competition for the layman, setting out a general model and examples from almost every subject dramatically simplifies the message. The work is interdisciplinary in that it involves economics, reasoning, decision-making and strategy theory. It includes several exercises and applications. It has practical results and is useful. The major subjects of this book are: individual; social games; firms; market; ethical questions. Each of these sections answers some of the relevant questions.

Any person can lead a better life. By setting goals, working to gain the necessary skills and motivation, gaining a deep understanding of the rules of the market, and finding an appropriate strategy for carrying out actions, everybody can reach any goal. Those with special skills, or who achieve great results, are often followed by much interest. Envy often stigmatizes quality and the benefits it brings. Nowadays, everybody can easily improve one's ability. This is the major message of this book, after all. Our difference from the animals comes from the opportunity to learn, not simply from individual trial and error. By making small efforts, anybody can lead a better life. No excuse is acceptable anymore.

9 798330 382798